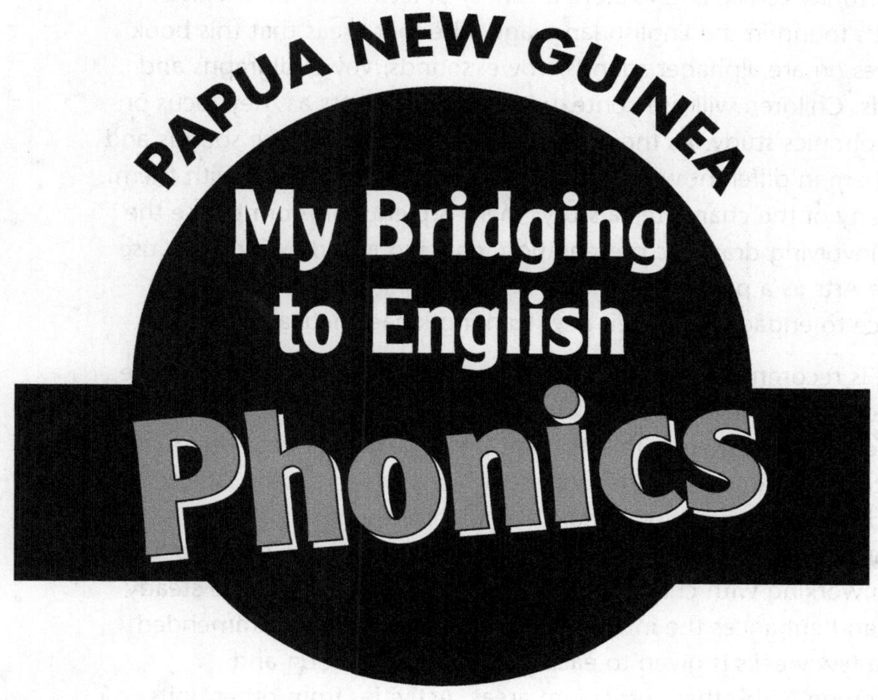

Darshini Jacob

To the Teacher

My Bridging to English: Phonics is designed to give children an opportunity to use and explore a variety of letter and letter cluster sounds found in the English language. The four areas that this book focuses on are alphabet sounds, vowel sounds, vowel digraphs and blends. Children will use contextually related chants as they focus on their phonics study. As the children hear and repeat these sounds and use them in different ways they will become more familiar with them. As many of the chants tell a story, there is plenty of room to use the Arts, involving dramatic presentation, dancing and drawing. This use of the Arts as a processing tool is vital, as it will give the children a chance to engage with their new learning kinaesthetically.

It is recommended that the children spend time in oral language first, discussing the chants and relating their personal experiences in connection with them. Objects related to a particular chant that can be accessed are useful visual representations which can be labelled and displayed. Discussion should also involve the rhyming words, the rhythm and the repetition they can hear. A useful instrument to have when working with chants is any sort of drum that keeps the steady beat and enhances the intonation of the words. It is recommended that a few weeks is given to each chant, in exploration and integration with other curriculum areas. Activities from other units can be adapted so that as much word study as possible accompanies the learning of each chant.

This resource is an important accompaniment to *My Bridging to English: Words in Context*, taking children into word study skills and developing their knowledge of sound–letter relationships within the English language.

Contents

Unit Summary

Chant activities	*Spelling outcomes*	*Phonic activities*	*Follow up activities*
Alphabet Chant Say each line of the chant, followed by the children, who clap with each three alphabet sounds. Talk about each sentence and draw the pictures. Teacher can sing the first part and children say the sounds. Sing the chant together, playing a drum to keep the beat. Discuss other words they know that also have the same letter sound.	To understand letter/sound relationships	Using the **Alphabet** chant, undertake the following activities: • Listen for the beginning sound, and write the beginning sound • Listen for the beginning sound, and circle the correct letter • Listen to the starting sound, write the missing word and draw a picture • Look at the picture, say the word, listen for the sound and write the letter • Look at the middle letter, colour the correct picture that matches the letter in the middle of the flower and cross out the others • Listen for the starting sound, find the starting letter and join them with a line. • Listen for which letter comes first, then second and write them all in the correct order. • Listen for the middle sound, say the middle letter and write the middle letter.	Collect objects from around the room and the yard, classifying and grouping them in alphabet groups. Mime a sentence of the chant. The others guess which line it is. Have big alphabet letters spread around the room. The children put them in order.
Nuts! Discuss nuts that children know and have eaten. Look at the picture and talk about the nuts in the hut. Say the chant together. Talk about and say the words that rhyme and sound the same. Write these down and look at the letter patterns.	To identify short vowel sounds	Using the **Nuts!** chant, undertake the following activities: • Look at the pictures, say each word, listen for the 'u' sound. Join them to the big U in the centre with a line if they do have a 'u' sound. • Say the vowel sounds, say the word for each picture, listen for the short vowel sound, and circle the words and the pictures if they have a short vowel sound. • Say the vowel sounds, look at each picture, listen for the missing vowel sound, and write in the missing vowel. • Say the vowel sound, find the picture with that sound, and join them together with a line • Roll the dice, say the name of the picture you land on, and say the sound of the vowel.	Bring a variety of nuts to school. Display them in the classroom to create a nutty atmosphere. Then eat the nuts.
Eating on an Island Look at the pictures. Ask children about their experiences of hunting/fishing and being hungry. Say the chant together. Discuss the sounds that were repeated through the song. Write down the letter sound they hear the most.	To identify long vowel sounds	Using the **Eating on an Island** chant, undertake the following activities: • Look at the pictures, listen for the vowel sound, and circle the words with a long 'o' sound. • Say the vowel sound, find the picture with that sound, and join them together with a line. • Say the vowel, say what each picture is, and cross out the pictures that do not have a long vowel sound. • Roll the dice; say the word for the picture that you land on, and then say what vowel the word uses.	Role-play the chant, either with one main character and the others singing, or the teacher singing while the children act out the chant. Cook an eel or fish together over a fire and eat it for lunch.

Chant activities	Spelling outcomes	Phonic activities	Follow up activities
Fruits Are Good Discuss fruits that the children know as they look at the pictures for this chant. Say the chant together. Talk about the sound they heard repeated through the chant. (The long 'e' sound) Write the long 'e' in the different ways it is represented on the board.	To identify long vowel sounds	Using the **Fruits Are Good** chant, undertake the following activity: • Look at the pictures, listen for the vowel sounds, find the four words with a long 'e' sound, and write them in the lines in the centre of the page.	Bring a variety of fruits into the classroom and discuss why they are healthy. Make a fruit salad and eat it together.
The Dog Ask the children to share their experiences with dogs. Say the chant together. Discuss the various sounds of 'o' they can hear and write the difference between the short and long 'o'.	To identify long vowel sounds	Using **The Dog** chant, undertake the following activity: • Look at the pictures, listen for the long 'o' sound, and join each word containing it with a line to the dog.	Play Dog and Bone—divide the class into two teams, and give each team member a number. (There will be a number 1 on each team, a number 2 on each team, and so on.) Place a bone in the centre of the room. The two teams stand on either side of the room. When a number is called, the two children with that number run to the bone and try to fetch it for their team to score a point.
Pineapples with Crowns Show the class a pineapple and children can discuss its appearance. Learn the chant and sing it with actions. Discuss and write the sounds the children heard repeated.	To identify 'ow', 'ou' and 'ack' blends	Using the **Pineapples with Crowns** chant, undertake the following activities: • Join the beginning, the middle 'ow' sound, and the ending to make four words. Join these words to the correct picture. • Follow the arrows to join the beginning, the 'ou' sound, and the ending to make words and write the words on the lines provided. • Look at the pictures and say what they are. Write the 'ack' blend for each word. Then use lines to join the words to the correct pictures.	Design and make crowns using materials from outdoors.
Juicy Sweet Mango Discuss the children's experiences with mangos. Look at a mango and describe it. Learn the chant, listening for the sounds they can hear through it. Write the word mango and show the children how it is two words.	To revise vowels	Using the **Juicy Sweet Mango** chant, undertake the following activity: • Fill in the missing vowels.	If mangos are readily available, make mango juice with chopped mango and water.

Chant activities	*Spelling outcomes*	*Phonic activities*	*Follow up activities*
Sugar Cane If sugar cane is easily accessible, bring in some for the children to look at and discuss. Learn the chant, listening for the sounds the children will hear repeated.	To identify 'ong' and 'in' words	Using the **Sugar Cane** chant, undertake the following activity: • Look at each word. If it is an 'ong' word, list it in the 'ong' column. If the word has 'in' in it, list it in the 'in' column. If it does not belong to either list, cross it out.	Eat sugar cane stick together.
The Poor Old Man Ask children where they have seen an old man. Learn the chant, listening for the sounds the children will hear repeated.	To identify the 'an' blend	Using **The Poor Old Man** chant, undertake the following activity: • Look at each picture and circle the ones that have the 'an' sound. Write the 'an' words in the pan.	Ask the children to perform a comic role-play of this chant.
Eat Some Peanuts Ask children what they know about peanuts and have some bunches on display. Learn the chant and discuss the sounds the children hear.	To identify the 'ch' and 'cr' blends	Using the **Eat Some Peanuts** chant, undertake the following activities: • Colour the chips that have the 'ch' sound in the words. Then circle the pictures that have a 'ch' sound. • Look at the pictures. Say each word and listen for the 'cr' sound. If the word has it, tick it. If the word doesn't have it, cross it out.	Boil and eat some peanuts together.
Sing Sing Time! Ask children to talk about their experiences of a sing sing. Look at the pictures and discuss them. Learn the chant and discuss the sounds they hear repeated.	To identify the 'ing' blend	Using the **Sing Sing Time!** chant, undertake the following activity: • Say the 'ing' sound and write it after each letter. Then say the whole word and write it under the correct picture.	Have a class sing sing—dressing up, doing dances and singing the chant.
The Pig Ask children to talk about their experiences of a mumu. Discuss the pictures. Learn the chant and talk about the story and the sounds they heard repeated.	To identify vowels and the 'ig' blend	Using **The Pig** chant, undertake the following activity: • Find words from the chant and pictures from the page to fit into the vowel pig.	Have a class mumu, or role-play the story of the hunt.
Playing in the Rain Ask children about their experiences of rain. Look at the pictures and discuss—explaining to those who aren't sure—what a train is. Learn the chant and talk about the story and the sounds the children heard repeated.	To identify the 'ain' blend	Using the **Playing in the Rain** chant, undertake the following activity: • Look at each picture, say the word and listen for an 'ain' sound. Circle the word and picture if it has an 'ain' sound. Try writing the words on the lines below.	Make human trains and play a racing game outside.
The Little Boy Ask children to talk about what toys they play with. Learn the chant and discuss the toys this boy had and the sounds they heard repeated.	To identify 'oy', 'uck', 'ar' and 'oat' blends	Using **The Little Boy** chant, undertake the following activity: • Match the picture with a drawing that has the same sound. Join them together with lines. Then fill in the missing vowels in the words below.	Ask children to bring in their toys and play with them together.

Chant activities	*Spelling outcomes*	*Phonic activities*	*Follow up activities*
Sleeping Sleeping Sleeping Snake Ask children to share their stories about and experiences with snakes. Learn the chant and talk about the story of the snake and the sounds they heard repeated.	To identify the 'ake' and 'ee' blends	Using the **Sleeping Sleeping Sleeping Snake** chant, undertake the following activity: • Match the letter blends with the correct pictures. • Colour the cakes that have an 'ake' word in them. • Match the correct word to its picture by joining them together with lines.	Make some snake mobiles by cutting a round piece of paper round and round inwards so that it spirals.
Police and Rascals Board Game	To identify initial letter sounds	Using the **Police and Rascals Board Game,** follow these instructions: • The first person to reach the rascals is the winner. Spaces that don't have an instruction on them have a letter instead. You must provide a word that begins with that letter before you can move on in the game. (You will need to take turns with a dice to play.)	
Good Morning Chant Learn the chant and get the children saying it each morning.	To combine learning with good manners	Using the **Good Morning Chant**, undertake the following activity: • Put actions to the chant so children learn to shake hands as they sing it.	
Goodbye Chant Learn the chant and get the children saying it each afternoon before they go home.	To combine learning with good manners	Using the **Goodbye Chant**, undertake the following activity: • Put actions to the chant so children learn to shake hands as they sing it.	
Clap Your Hands and Two Steps Forward These chants are for the children to do whenever they need to stretch and move around or when you have a few spare minutes.	To combine learning with exercise	Using the **Clap Your Hands** and the **Two Steps Forward** chants, undertake the following activity: • Write these chants on large pieces of paper. Ask children to do hand or foot prints around the chants, and display them on the wall.	
Word List This list is for children to refer to once they have used and become familiar with the words from each chant.	To re-enforce vocabulary learnt in this book	Using the **Word List**, undertake the following activity: • Write out selected words from the list and display them on the wall. These could be commonly used words, or ones that the children find more challenging.	Use the lists for reading and spelling activities and games, as well as for reference when writing.

Alphabet Chant

Axe on an **a**nt **a a a**

Baby in a **b**ilum **b b b**

Cat on a **c**ar **c c c**

Dog is **d**riving **d d d**

Extra **e**ggs **e e e**

Frying **f**ish **f f f**

Girl on the **g**rass **g g g**

Hearts on a **h**ouse **h h h**

Itchy **i**nsects **i i i**

Juice is **j**umping **j j j**

Kaukau and **k**undu **k k k**

Light the **l**amp **l l l**

Mumu on a **m**ountain **m m m**

Nuts in a **n**est **n n n**

Orange on an **o**ctopus **o o o**

Pigs are **p**laying **p p p**

Quiet says the **q**ueen **q q q**

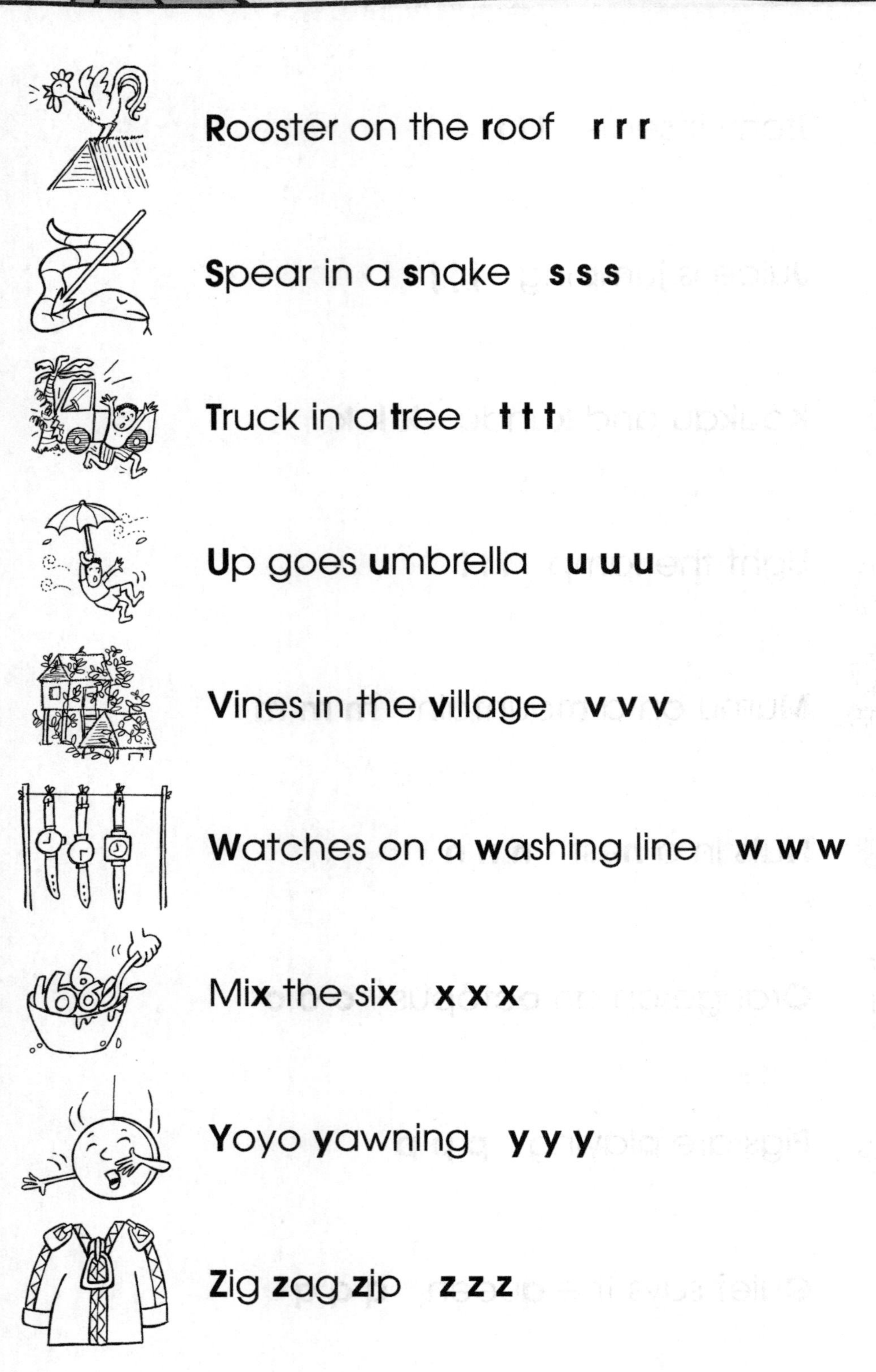

Rooster on the **r**oof **r r r**

Spear in a **s**nake **s s s**

Truck in a **t**ree **t t t**

Up goes **u**mbrella **u u u**

Vines in the **v**illage **v v v**

Watches on a **w**ashing line **w w w**

Mi**x** the si**x** **x x x**

Yoyo **y**awning **y y y**

Zig **z**ag **z**ip **z z z**

Unit 1

Write what I start with!

Look at the picture, say what it is, listen for the beginning sound, and write it down.

axe ___

house ___

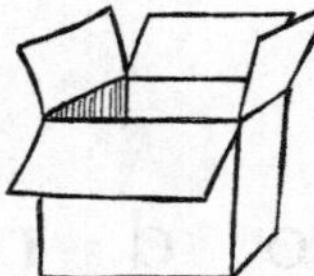

box ___

insect ___

car ___

juice ___

dog ___

kundu drum ___

egg ___

lamp ___

fish ___

mountain ___

grass ___

nest ___

Alphabet Activity 1
Area of focus: Initial letter sound

Circle the correct letter

Look at the picture, say what it is, listen for its beginning sound, and circle the correct letter.

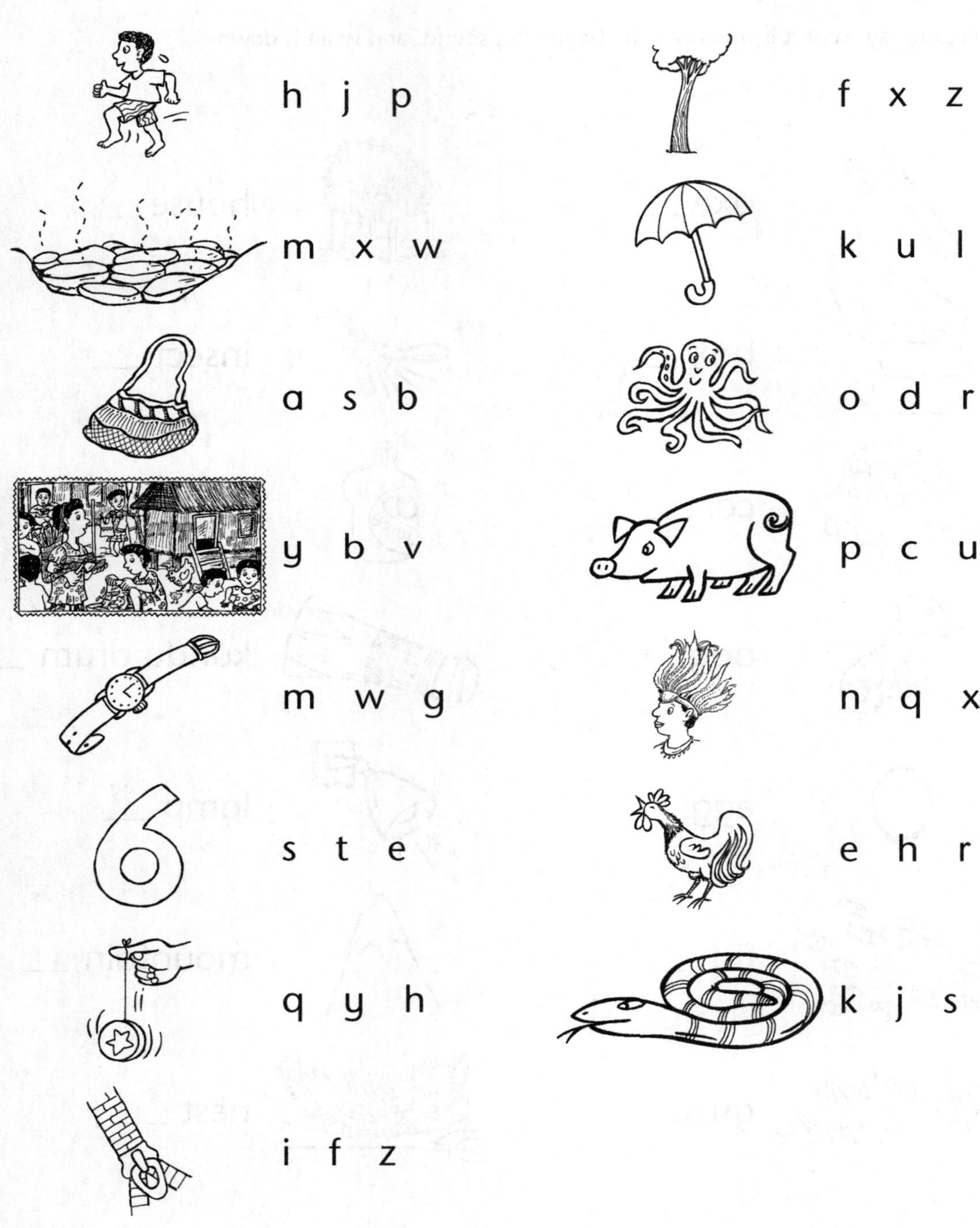

Alphabet Activity 2
Area of focus: Initial letter sound

What's missing?

Read the alphabet chant, read each phrase, listen to the starting sounds, write the missing letters, and draw your own picture.

Boy in a __ilum 

Vines in the __illage 

Watches on a __ashing line 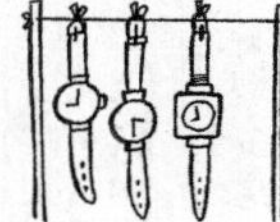

Man on a __ountain 

Happy __earts 

Spear in a __nake 

Cat on a __ar 

Rooster on a __oof 

Pigs are __laying 

Frying __ish 

Alphabet Activity 3
Area of focus: Initial letter sound

Write what I start with!

Look at the picture, say the word, listen for the beginning sound, and write the letter.

Alphabet Activity 4
Area of focus: Initial letter sound

Match me!

Look at the picture, listen for the beginning sound, find the starting letter in the next column, and join the matching word and picture together with a line.

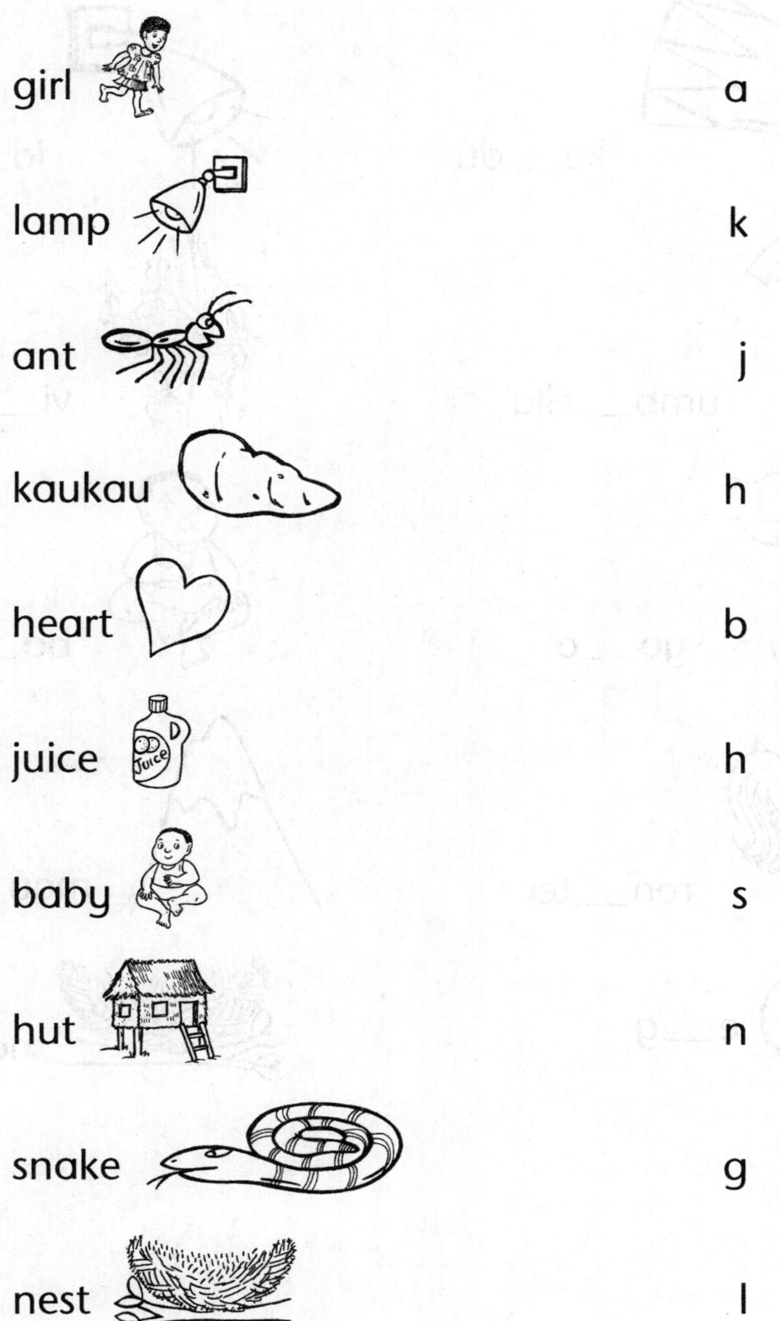

girl	a
lamp	k
ant	j
kaukau	h
heart	b
juice	h
baby	s
hut	n
snake	g
nest	l

Alphabet Activity 5
Area of focus: Initial letter sound

Missing middle

Look at the picture, listen for the middle sound, say the middle letter, and write it in the word.

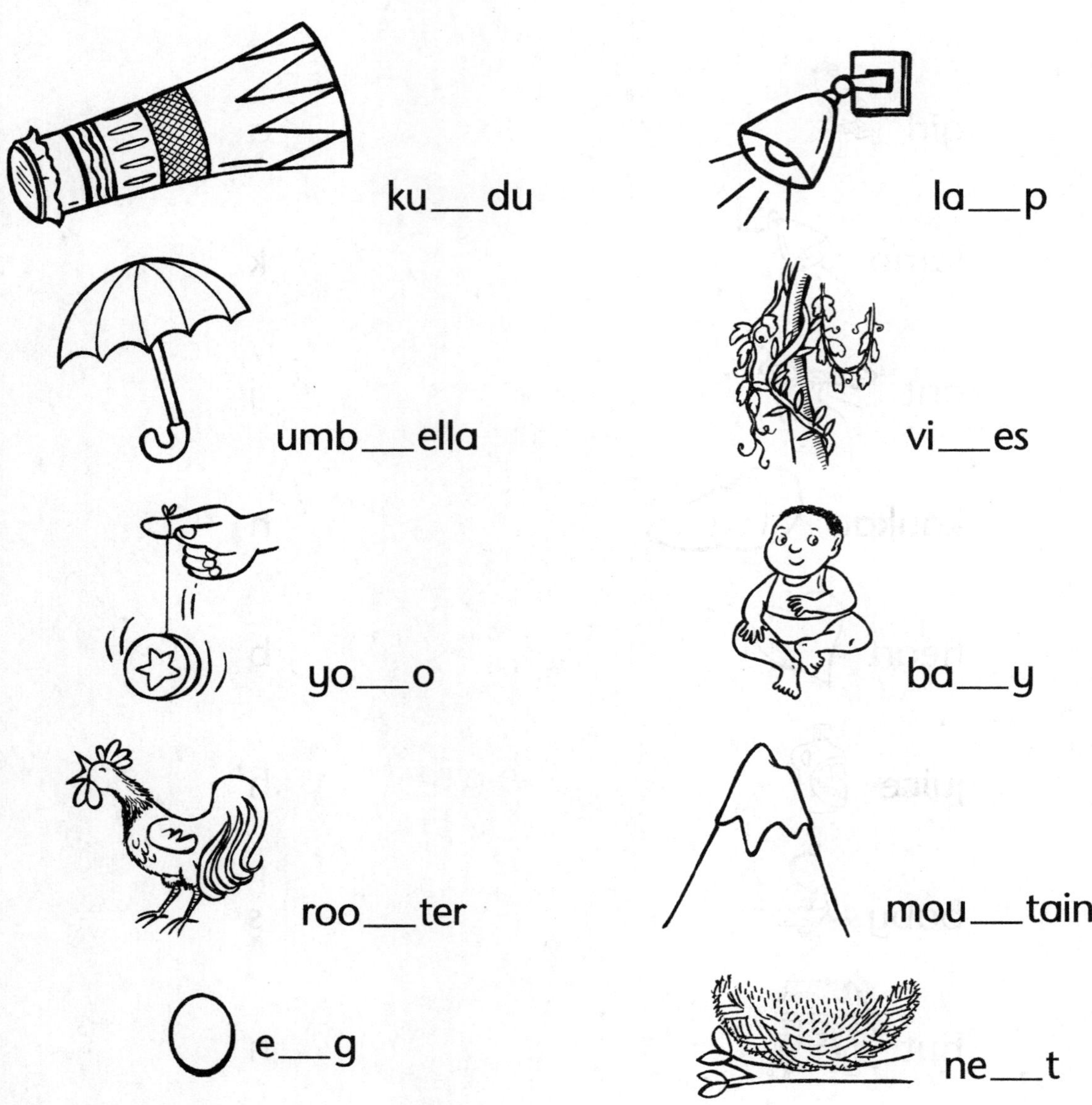

ku___du

la___p

umb___ella

vi___es

yo___o

ba___y

roo___ter

mou___tain

e___g

ne___t

Alphabet Activity 6
Area of focus: Middle letter sound

Nuts!

In a hut
In a hut
Sitting on the hill

There are nuts
There are nuts
My tummy needs a fill!

Peanuts
Peanuts
All over the floor

Betel nut
Betel nut
Hanging on the door

Coconuts
Coconuts
Sitting on the shelf

In this hut
In this hut
I shall feed myself!

Unit 2

U, where are you?

Look at the pictures, and say each word, listening for the 'u' sound. Join them to the big U in the centre with a line if they do have a 'u' sound.

Vowel Activity 1
Area of focus: 'u' sound

Can you hear me?

Say the vowel sounds, say the word for each picture, listen for the short vowel sound, and circle the words and the pictures if they have a short vowel sound.

a	e	i	o	u

bike

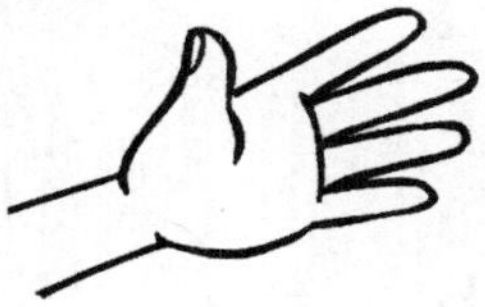

hand

pot

rooster

bee

cat

sheep

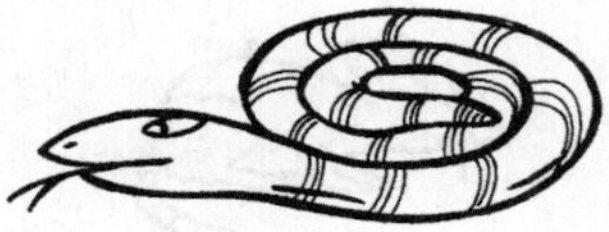

snake

frog

pig

Vowel Activity 2
Area of focus: Short vowel sounds

Lost in the middle!

Say the vowel sounds, look at each picture, listen for the missing vowel sound, and write in the missing vowel.

a	e	i	o	u

h__t

d__g

ch__cken

b__lum

p__n

__nt

b__x

r__t

n__st

p__g

Vowel Activity 3
Area of focus: Short vowel sounds

Match me!

Say the vowel sound, find the picture with that sound, and join them together with a line.

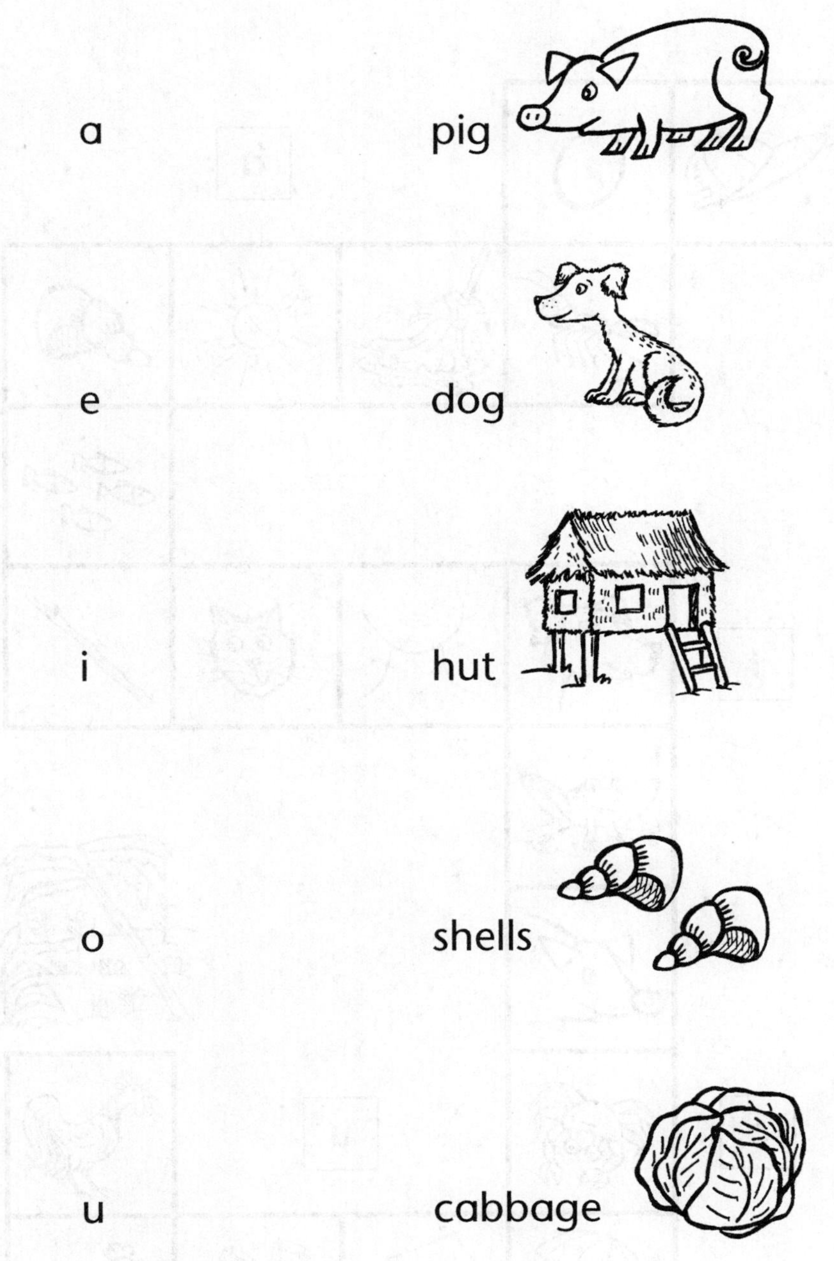

Vowel Activity 4
Area of focus: Short vowel sounds

Hut to garden game

Roll the dice, say the name of the picture you land on, and say the sound of the vowel.

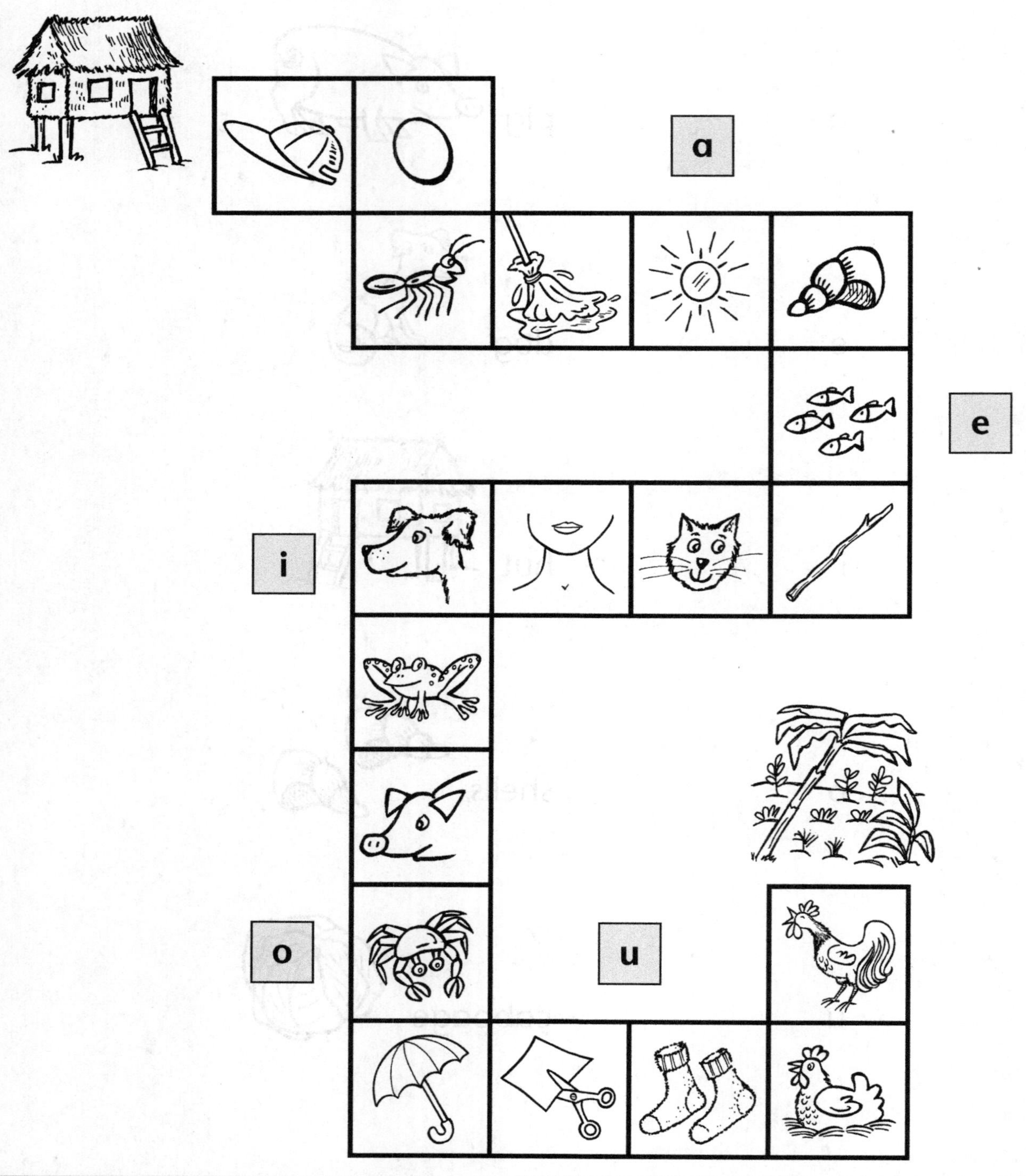

Vowel Activity 5
Area of focus: Short vowel sounds

Eating on an Island

I am on an island
I need to eat
Oh! Oh!
Oh! Oh!

I see an eel
I spear and take it
Oh! Oh!
Oh! Oh!

I use the lighter
I make a fire
Oh! Oh!
Oh! Oh!

I cook the eel
I open my mouth
Oh! Oh!
Oh! Oh!

I eat the meat
My meal is over
Oh! Oh!
Oh! Oh!

I go to sleep
After eating my meat
Oh! Oh!
Oh! Oh!

Unit 3

Oh! Where are you?

Look at the pictures, listen for the vowel sound, and circle the words with a long 'o' sound.

coconut

telephone

possum

book

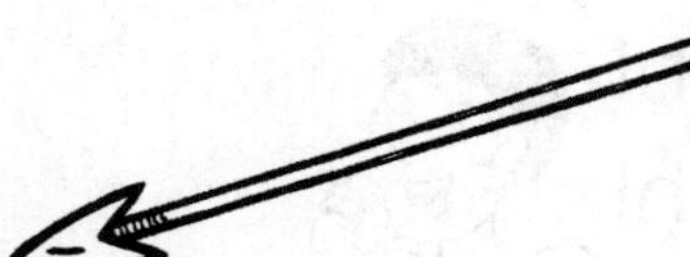

flower

stones

spear

ice cream cone

Vowel Activity 6
Area of focus: Long 'o' sound

Match me!

Say the vowel sound, find the picture with that sound, and join them together with a line.

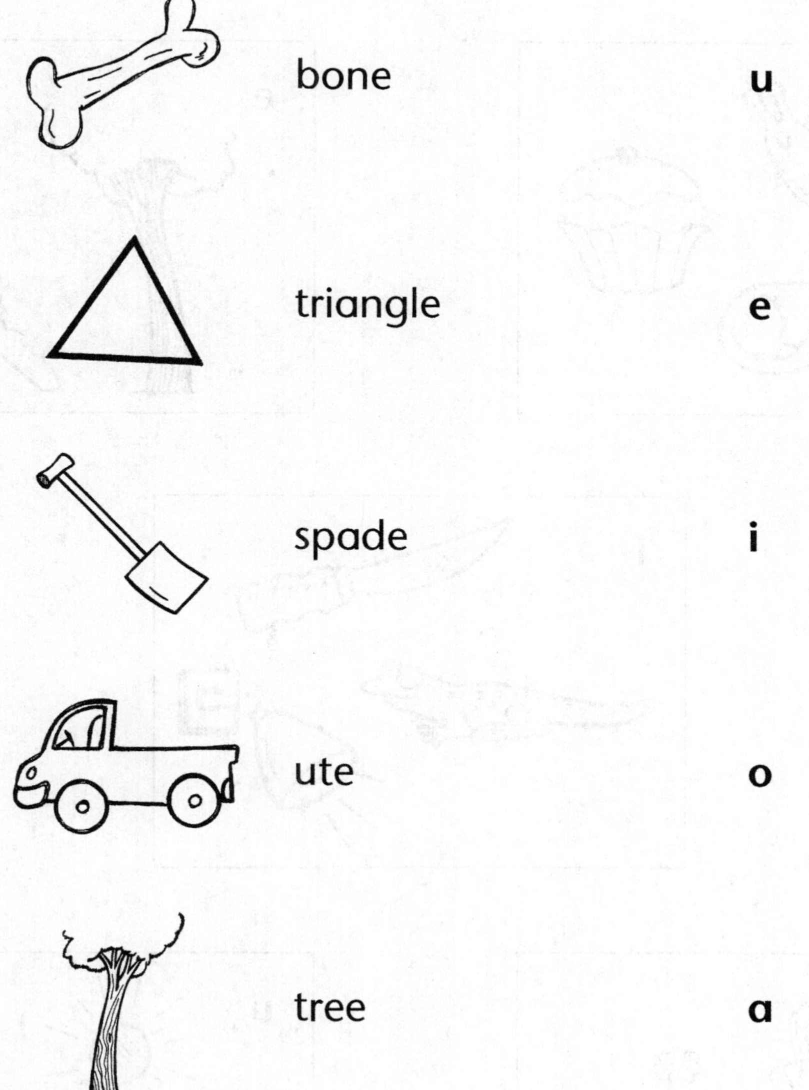

Not you!

Say the vowel, say what each picture is, and cross out the pictures that do not have a long vowel sound.

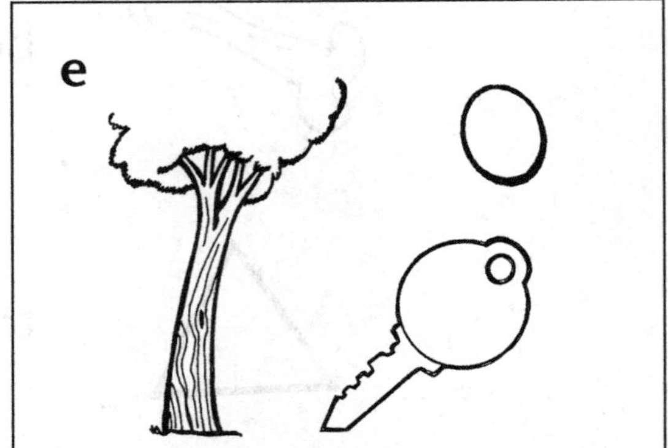

Vowel Activity 8
Area of focus: Long vowel sounds

School to home game

Roll the dice; say the word for the picture that you land on, and then say what vowels the word uses.

Vowel Activity 9
Area of focus: Long vowel sounds

Fruits Are Good

Fruits are good
Fruits are good

Good for me
Good for me

Fruits are good
Fruits are good

Very healthy
Very healthy

Fruits are good
Fruits are good

In my body
In my body

Unit 4

Which four have a long 'e'?

Look at the pictures, listen for the vowel sounds, find the four words with a long 'e' sound, and write them on the lines in the centre of the page.

pot

bee

sea

vine

possum

money

tree

kundu

Vowel Activity 10
Area of focus: Long 'e' sound

The Dog

Dog is barking
See his bones
Dog is howling
He has no home

Dog is standing
All alone
Dog is sitting
Near the stones

Come on Doggy
Come with me
I will give you
An ice cream cone!

Unit 5

Give the dog an 'o'!

Look at the pictures, listen for the long 'o' sound, and join each word containing it with a line to the dog.

Vowel Activity 11
Area of focus: Long 'o' sound

Pineapples with Crowns

I was going to town

Over the hills

Up and down

I was going to the market

Carrying pineapples with crowns

Ow! Ow! Ow!

They poked into my back!

Ow! Ow! Ow!

Heavy bilum, heavy sack!

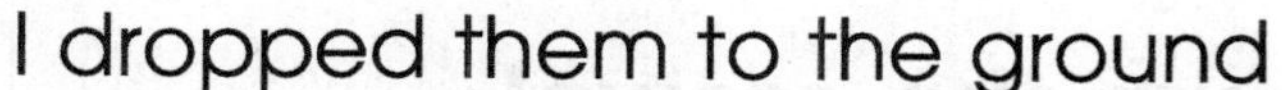

I dropped them to the ground

It was dirty

It was brown

Can I sell them here?

I look here, there and around

No! No! No!

No one to be found

Bilum up (clap, clap, clap)

On my head (clap, clap, clap)

Keep going to the town

Over the hills

Up and down

Keep going to the market

Carrying pineapples with crowns.

Unit 6

Going down the crown!

Join the beginning, the middle 'ow' sound and the ending to make four words. Write these words next to the correct picture.

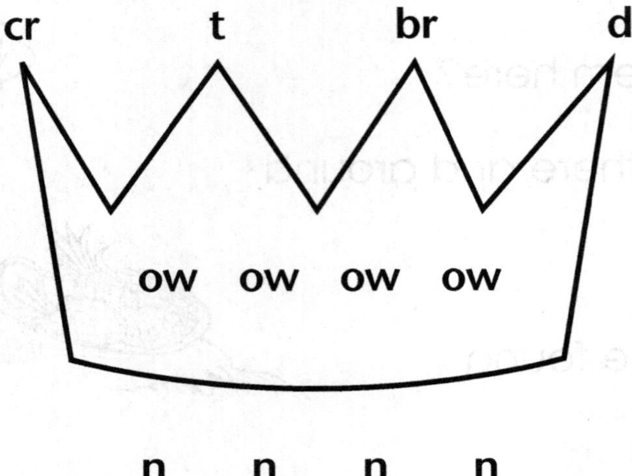

n n n n

____

____

____

____

Blend Digraph Activity 12
Area of focus: 'ow' blend

Follow the arrow out

Follow the arrows to make words. Join a beginning sound with the 'ou' blend, then choose the ending that will make a proper word. Write the words on the lines provided.

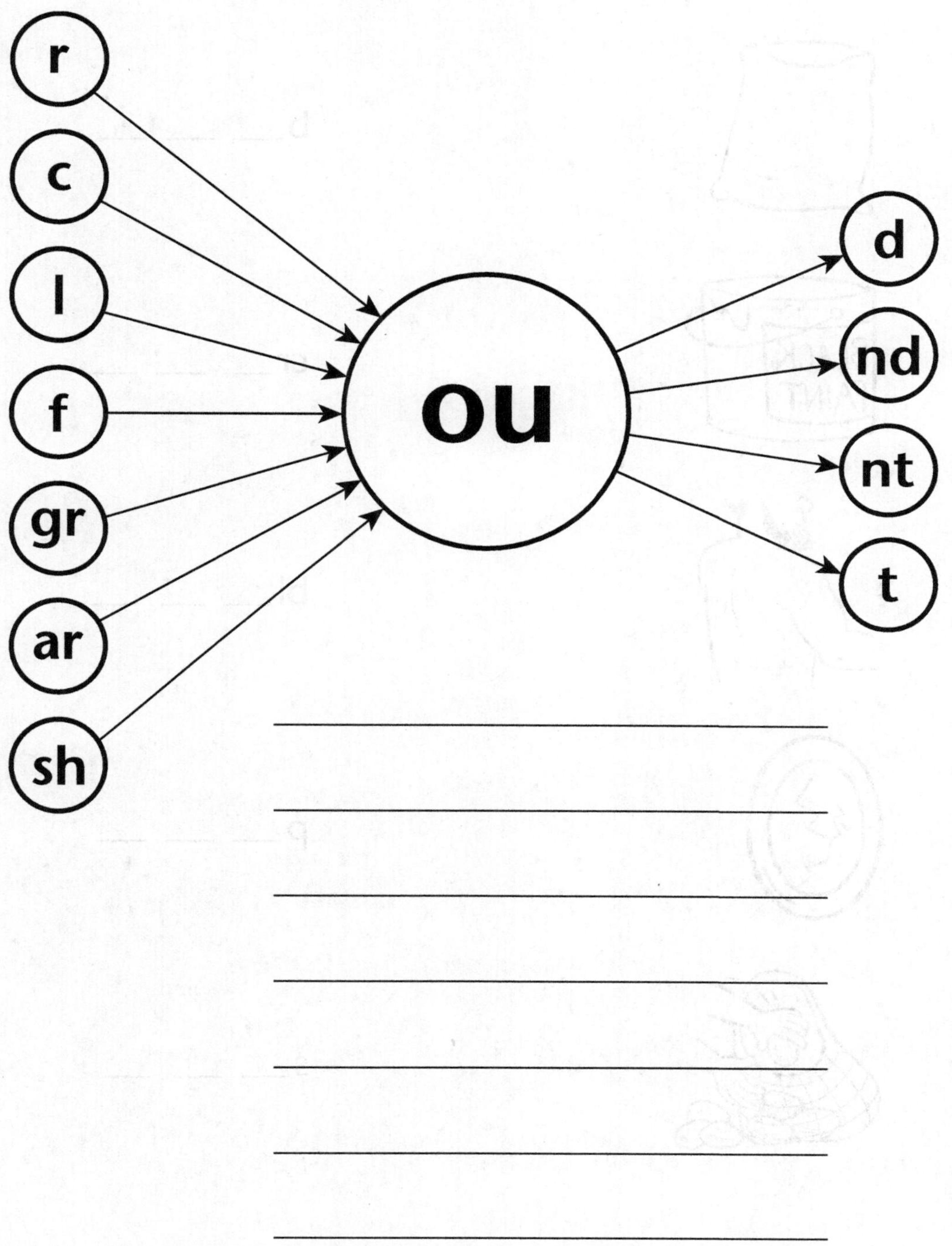

Blend Digraph Activity 13
Area of focus: 'ou' blend

Put them back!

Look at the pictures and say what they are. Write the 'ack' blend for each word. Then use lines to join the words to the correct pictures.

b___ ___ ___

cr___ ___ ___

bl___ ___ ___

p___ ___ ___

s___ ___ ___

Blend Digraph Activity 14
Area of focus: 'ack' blend

Juicy Sweet Mango

Juicy sweet mango
Lying on the ground
Juicy sweet mango
That's what I have found
Peel the skin off
Take a big bite
Juicy sweet mango
You are so nice!

Unit 7

Lost vowels

Fill in the missing vowels in these words.

Juicy sw__ __t mango

Lying on the gr__ __nd

Juicy sw__ __t mango

That's what I have f__ __nd

P__ __l the skin off

Take a big bite

Juicy sw__ __t mango

You are so nice!

Vowel Activity 15
Area of focus: Vowels

Sugar Cane

Sugar cane is sweet
Sugar cane is long
Sugar cane is chewy
Makes my teeth strong!

Sugar cane grows tall
Sugar cane is thin
When you finish chewing
Put it in the bin!

Unit 8

Where do you belong?

Look at each word. If it is an 'ong' word, list it in the 'ong' column. If the word has an 'in' in it, list it in the 'in' column. If it does not belong to either list, cross it out.

strong	bat	bin	fit	win	long	song
yes	this	fin	thin	man	pin	

ong	in

Blend Digraph Activity 16
Area of focus: 'ong' and 'in' blends

The Poor Old Man

The poor old man
Whose name is Dan
The poor old man
He ran ran ran
The poor old man
With his frying pan
His cooker and his kerosene can
The poor old man
Was chased by a van
I'm sure it was a rascal gang!

Unit 9

Can you find 'an'?

Look at each picture, and circle those that have the 'an' blend. Write the 'an' words in the pan.

Blend Digraph Activity 17
Area of focus: 'an' blend

Eat Some Peanuts

Eat some peanuts

Crunch, crunch, crunch

Eat some sugar cane

Munch, munch, munch

Drink some juice

Slurp, slurp, slurp

That was delicious

Burp, burp, burp!

Unit 10

Choose a 'ch'!

Colour the chips that have the sound 'ch' in the words. Then circle the pictures that have a 'ch' sound.

Blend Digraph Activity 18
Area of focus: 'ch' blend

Cross or tick?

Look at the pictures. Say each word and listen for the 'cr' blend. If the word begins with 'cr', tick it. If the word doesn't begin with 'cr', cross it out.

Blend Digraph Activity 19
Area of focus: 'cr' blend

Sing Sing Time!

What's happening?
What's happening?
At the sing sing?
At the sing sing?
People dance and hit the drum

Dum dee dee
Dum dee dee
Dum dee dee
Dum!

Grass skirts move from side to side
See the bodies jump and glide
Singing, shouting, sounds of pride
Come on everyone, it's sing sing time!

Unit 11

Can you hear 'ing' ring?

Say the blend 'ing' and write it after each letter. Then say the whole word and write it under the correct picture.

ing

k___ ___ ___   s___ ___ ___

r___ ___ ___   w___ ___ ___

______________________   ______________________

______________________   ______________________

Blend Digraph Activity 20
Area of focus: 'ing' blend

The Pig

See the pig
See the pig
See the very big fat pig

Catch the pig
Catch the pig
Catch the very big fat pig

Now let's dig
Now let's dig
Now let's dig a hole that's big

Kill the pig
Kill the pig
Kill the very big fat pig

Drop the pig
Drop the pig
In the hole that's very big

Eat the pig
Eat the pig
Lunch is very very big!

Unit 12

A big vowel pig

Look at the picture, say what it is, and write the missing letter.

Blend Digraph Activity 21
Area of focus: Vowels and 'ig' blend

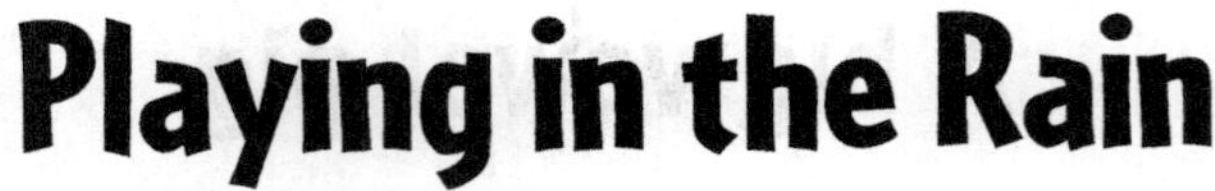

Playing in the Rain

Playing in the rain
Making a train
Didn't see the drain
Oh no! I have a pain!

My ankle has a sprain
My clothes are all stained

Lying in the rain
Broken crying train
Train with a sprain
Lying in the drain!

Unit 13

Which ain't 'ain'?

Look at each picture, say the word and listen for an 'ain' sound. Circle the picture if it has an 'ain' sound. Try writing the words on the lines below.

Blend Digraph Activity 22
Area of focus: 'ain' blend

The Little Boy

The little boy
Who is playing with his toys
Who is playing with his toys . . .

He has a truck
Oh! Its wheels are stuck!

He has a car
Oh! It's gone too far!

He has a boat
Oh! It cannot float!

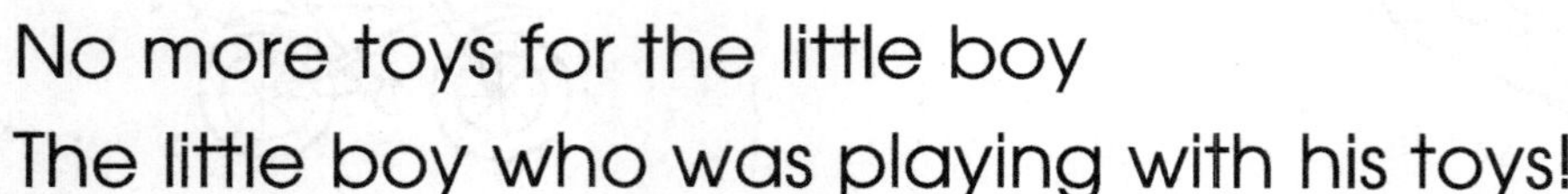

No more toys for the little boy
The little boy who was playing with his toys!

Unit 14

What sounds like me?

Match each picture with a drawing that has the same sound. Join them together with lines. Then fill in the missing vowels in the words below.

truck 

goat 

car

boy 

toy 

duck 

boat 

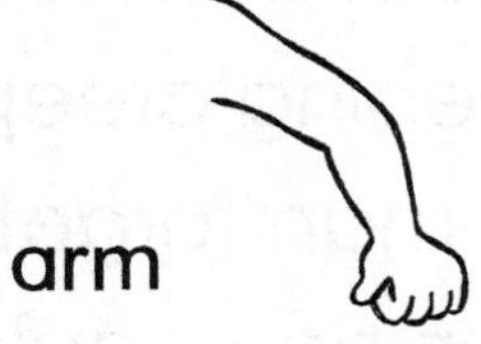
arm

He has a tr___ck.

H___ has a car.

He h___s a boat.

Oh, ___t cannot float.

Blend Digraph Activity 23
Area of focus: 'oy', 'uck', 'ar', 'oat' blends

Sleeping Sleeping Sleeping Snake

Sleeping sleeping sleeping snake
Make sure he doesn't wake!
Creeping creeping creeping snake
Likes to eat the chocolate cake!
Scary scary scary snake
Looking at the mother shake
Scaly scaly scaly snake
Likes to curl up and sunbake
Peeping peeping peeping snake
Lives in bushes by the lake
Creeping creeping creeping snake
The man forgot to press the brake
Sleeping sleeping sleeping snake
You will never ever wake

Unit 15

Can you hear me?

Find the words in the chant and write the missing letters. Match the letter blends with the correct pictures.

br ___ ___ ___

ch ___ ___ ___ ___ ___ ___ ___ ___ ___ ___ ___

cr ___ ___ ___

pr ___ ___ ___

sc ___ ___ ___

sh ___ ___ ___

sl ___ ___ ___

Blend Digraph Activity 24
Area of focus: Blends

What will you take?

Colour the cakes that have an 'ake' blend in them.

Blend Digraph Activity 25
Area of focus: 'ake' blends

Let's meet!

Match each word to the correct picture by joining them together with lines.

sleep

feed

creep

feet

meet

seed

weed

peel

wheel

kneel

Blend Digraph Activity 26
Area of focus: 'ee' words

Police and Rascals Board Game

Held up by the BRA in Arawa, miss 2 turns

The first person to reach the rascals is the winner. Spaces that don't have an instruction on them have a letter instead. You must provide a word that begins with that letter before you can move on in the game. (You will need to take turns with a dice to play.)

Start Port Moresby	a	Stop for a swim in Alotau, miss a turn	b	c	Get a free boat ride, move forward 3 spaces	d

w	x	Catch malaria in Vanimo, miss 2 turns	Sago from Wewak gives you strength, move forward 2 spaces	y	z
Get a free plane ride from Daru, move ahead 2 spaces					**Finish:** You catch the rascals hiding in Lorengau!
v					

u	t	Stop for a sing sing in Mt Hagen, miss a turn	s	r	PMV driver gives you a ride, move forward 4 spaces	q

Alphabet Activity 27

e	Stop to see a volcano in Rabaul, miss a turn	f	g	Clues are given to you by Trobriand Islanders, move forward 3 spaces	h	i

j

Stop for a sing sing in Popondetta, miss 2 turns

Called back to Port Moresby for business, go back to Start

k

l

Lorengau

Wewak

Rabaul

Mount Hagen

Arawa

Kerema

Kokoda

Trobriand Is.

Popondetta

Daru

PORT MORESBY

Alotau

N

W

E

S

Lost on the Kokoda trail, miss a turn	Find a shortcut through the mountain ranges, move forward 5 spaces	p	o	Get bitten by a crocodile in Kerema, miss a turn	n	m

Short rhymes to say through the day

Good Morning Chant

Good morning!

Good morning!

What a beautiful day

Good morning!

Good morning!

Let's work and play!

Goodbye Chant

Goodbye

Goodbye

It's time to go

Goodbye

Goodbye

See you tomorrow

GOODBYE!

I Can Have Fun Chant

I have hands and I have feet

I have a heart and lungs that breathe

I can jump and I can run

I can clap and I can have fun!

Clap Your Hands Chant

Clap your hands and stamp your feet

Blink your eyes and make palms meet

Stretching up and stretching down

Touch the sky and touch the ground!

Two Steps Forward Chant

Two steps forward

Two steps back

Touch your toes

And that is that!

Turn to the left

Now turn to the right

Back to the middle

Sitting nice and quiet!

Word List

A
all
alone
ankle
ant
arm
around
axe

B
baby
back
bag
barking
bat
beautiful
bee
betel nut
bicycle
big
bike
bilum
bin
bite
black
blink
boat
body
bone
book
box

boy
brakes
breathe
broken
brown
burp
bus
bushes

C
cabbage
cake
can
cap
car
carry
cat
catch
chain
chase
cheese
chewy
chicken
chip
chips
chocolate
chop
clap
clothes
cloud
coconut

come
cone
cook
cooker
count
crab
crack
creep
creeping
crocodile
cross
crown
crunch
cry
crying
cucumber
curl
cut

D
dance
day
delicious
dig
dirty
dog
door
down
drain
drainpipe
drink

driving
drop
drum
duck

E
eat
eel
egg
ever
everyone
extra
eye

F
fan
fat
feed
feet
fill
fin
fire
fish
fit
float
floor
flower
fly
forgot
forward
found

frog
fruit
frying pan
fun

G
gang
gecko
girl
give
glide
go
goat
going
gone
good
goodbye
grass
ground

H
hand
hang
have
head
healthy
heart
hen
here
hill
hit
hole
home
house

howling
hut

I
ice cream
insect
island
itchy

J
jellyfish
juice
jogging
jump

K
kaukau
keep
kerosene can
key
kill
king
kite
kneel
knife
kundu drum

L
lake
lamp
left
light
lighter
like

little
lizard
lock
log
long
loud
lungs
lying

M
man
mango
market
meal
meat
meet
middle
mix
money
mop
more
morning
mother
mountain
mouth
move
mumu
munch
myself

N
name
neck
nest

never
nice
now
nuts

O
octopus
old
open
orange
out
over

P
pack
pain
paint
paintbrush
palms
pan
peanut
peel
peeping
pencil
people
pig
pin
pineapple
play
playing
poke
poor
possum
pot